Table of Contents

Chapter 1: Introduction to China's AI Revolution 2
  The Rise of Artificial Intelligence in China 2
  Overview of China's AI Strategy 3
  Key Players in China's AI Industry 5
Chapter 2: China's Government Initiatives in AI 6
  National Development Plan for AI 6
  Investment in AI Research and Development 7
  AI Education and Talent Development 9
Chapter 3: Leading AI Companies in China 11
  Baidu: Pioneer in AI Technology 11
  Alibaba: Innovations in AI Applications 12
  Tencent: Advancements in AI Research 13
Chapter 4: Challenges and Opportunities in China's AI Evolution 15
  Ethical and Regulatory Issues in AI Development 15
  International Collaboration and Competition in AI 16
  Potential Impact of China's AI Dominance on Global Economy 18
Chapter 5: Future Outlook for China's AI Industry 20
  Predictions for China's Position in AI by 2030 20
  Potential Implications of China's AI Revolution on Society 21
  Recommendations for Businesses and Governments in Response to China's AI Ambition 23
Chapter 6: Conclusion 24
  Key Takeaways from China's AI Revolution 24
  Final Thoughts on the Road to 2030 25

Chapter 1: Introduction to China's AI Revolution

The Rise of Artificial Intelligence in China

China's rapid rise in the field of artificial intelligence has been nothing short of remarkable. With the government making significant investments in AI research, education, and application, the country is well on its way to becoming a global leader in this cutting-edge technology by the year 2030. The Chinese government's commitment to AI is evident in its "Next Generation Artificial Intelligence Development Plan," which outlines ambitious goals for the development of AI in the country.

Leading the charge in China's AI revolution are tech giants like Baidu, Alibaba, and Tencent. These companies have been at the forefront of AI technology development, investing heavily in research and development to stay ahead of the curve. Baidu, for example, has been working on autonomous driving technology and natural language processing, while Alibaba has been focused on using AI to enhance e-commerce and cloud computing services. Tencent, on the other hand, has been leveraging AI to improve its social media and gaming platforms.

One of the key factors driving China's AI ambition is the country's vast pool of data. With over 800 million internet users and a thriving tech industry, China has access to a wealth of data that can be used to train AI algorithms. This data advantage has allowed Chinese companies to develop AI technologies that are tailored to the unique needs of the Chinese market, giving them a competitive edge in the global AI race.

In addition to data, China's strong focus on education and research has also played a crucial role in driving the country's AI revolution. The Chinese government has been investing heavily in AI education and training programs, with the goal of producing a skilled workforce that can drive innovation in the field. Universities and research institutions in China have also been conducting cutting-edge research in AI, leading to breakthroughs in areas such as computer vision, natural language processing, and robotics.

As China continues to make strides in AI technology, it is clear that the country is well-positioned to become a global leader in this field by 2030. With the government's support, tech giants driving innovation, and a strong foundation in data and research, China's AI revolution is set to reshape industries and drive economic growth in the coming years. For those interested in learning more about China's plan to dominate the AI landscape, "China's AI Revolution: The Road to 2030" provides a comprehensive overview of the country's ambitions and the steps it is taking to achieve them.

Overview of China's AI Strategy

China's AI strategy is a comprehensive plan aimed at positioning the country as a global leader in artificial intelligence by the year 2030. This ambitious goal has been backed by significant investments from the Chinese government, with a strong focus on education, research, and application of AI technologies. By leveraging the power of AI, China aims to drive innovation, boost economic growth, and enhance its overall competitiveness on the world stage.

One of the key pillars of China's AI strategy is the development of a robust ecosystem for AI education and research. The government has been actively promoting AI education at all levels, from primary schools to universities, in order to cultivate a new generation of AI talent. Additionally, China has established numerous research institutions and innovation hubs dedicated to advancing AI technologies and fostering collaboration between academia and industry.

Leading Chinese tech companies such as Baidu, Alibaba, and Tencent have emerged as key players in the country's AI landscape. These companies have been at the forefront of developing cutting-edge AI technologies and applications, spanning a wide range of industries including healthcare, finance, and transportation. Through strategic partnerships and investments, these companies are driving the adoption of AI across various sectors and accelerating China's progress towards its AI goals.

China's AI strategy also includes a strong emphasis on the ethical and responsible deployment of AI technologies. The government has put in place regulations and guidelines to ensure that AI is used in a way that benefits society and upholds fundamental rights and values. By promoting transparency, accountability, and fairness in AI development and deployment, China aims to build trust and confidence in AI technologies among its citizens and the international community.

In conclusion, China's AI strategy is a multifaceted approach that encompasses education, research, application, and ethical considerations. With the government's strong support and the active involvement of leading tech companies, China is well-positioned to achieve its goal of becoming a global leader in AI by 2030. By leveraging the power of AI, China is poised to drive innovation, spur economic growth, and shape the future of technology in the years to come.

Key Players in China's AI Industry

In the fast-paced world of artificial intelligence (AI), China has emerged as a key player with ambitious plans to become the global leader in the industry by 2030. The Chinese government has been heavily investing in AI, with a focus on education, research, and application. This strategic approach has put China on the map as a force to be reckoned with in the AI revolution.

Leading the charge in China's AI industry are tech giants Baidu, Alibaba, and Tencent, commonly referred to as the BAT companies. These companies have been at the forefront of AI technology development in China, leveraging their vast resources and expertise to drive innovation and shape the future of AI. From autonomous vehicles to facial recognition technology, Baidu, Alibaba, and Tencent are shaping the way AI is used in various industries.

Baidu, often referred to as the Google of China, has been a pioneer in AI research and development. The company's deep learning platform, Apollo, is leading the way in autonomous driving technology, while its AI-powered search engine is revolutionizing the way people search for information online.

Alibaba, the e-commerce giant, has been using AI to enhance customer experience, optimize logistics, and personalize recommendations for users. Tencent, known for its popular messaging app WeChat, has been leveraging AI to improve user engagement and develop innovative products and services.

These key players in China's AI industry are not only driving technological advancements but also shaping government policies and regulations surrounding AI development. As China continues to invest heavily in AI research and development, these companies will play a crucial role in realizing the country's ambition to become the world leader in AI by 2030. With their vast resources, expertise, and strategic partnerships, Baidu, Alibaba, and Tencent are leading the charge in China's AI revolution, setting the stage for a future where AI technology is at the forefront of innovation and progress.

Chapter 2: China's Government Initiatives in AI

National Development Plan for AI

China's National Development Plan for AI is a comprehensive strategy aimed at positioning the country as a global leader in artificial intelligence by the year 2030. This ambitious plan includes significant investments in education, research, and the practical application of AI technology across various industries. The Chinese government has made AI a top priority, recognizing its potential to drive economic growth and innovation in the coming decades.

One of the key pillars of China's National Development Plan for AI is the emphasis on developing a skilled workforce capable of driving the country's AI ambitions forward. This includes increasing funding for AI education and training programs, as well as attracting top talent from around the world. By investing in human capital, China aims to build a strong foundation for the development and deployment of cutting-edge AI technologies.

In addition to investing in education, China's National Development Plan for AI also focuses on fostering a vibrant research ecosystem. The government has allocated significant resources to support AI research projects, collaborations, and partnerships between academia, industry, and government agencies. This collaborative approach is designed to accelerate the pace of innovation and ensure that China remains at the forefront of AI technology development.

Leading Chinese tech companies such as Baidu, Alibaba, and Tencent are playing a crucial role in driving the implementation of China's National Development Plan for AI. These companies are investing heavily in AI research and development, as well as incorporating AI technologies into their products and services. By leveraging their expertise and resources, these companies are helping to accelerate the adoption of AI across various sectors of the economy.

Overall, China's National Development Plan for AI represents a bold vision for the country's future. By investing in education, research, and application of AI technology, China aims to become a global leader in artificial intelligence by 2030. With the support of the government and leading tech companies, China is well-positioned to realize its AI ambitions and shape the future of the technology landscape.

Investment in AI Research and Development

China's ambitious plan to become the world leader in artificial intelligence by 2030 has required significant investments in research and development. The Chinese government has allocated substantial resources to support the growth of AI technology, with a particular focus on education, research, and application. This investment has helped to propel China to the forefront of the global AI race, with companies like Baidu, Alibaba, and Tencent leading the charge in developing cutting-edge AI technologies.

One of the key areas of focus for China's investment in AI research and development has been in education. The government has implemented programs to cultivate a new generation of AI talent, providing funding for AI-related courses and research projects at universities across the country. This focus on education has helped to ensure that China has a steady supply of skilled AI professionals to drive innovation and development in the field.

In addition to education, China has also invested heavily in AI research. The government has established research institutions and laboratories dedicated to advancing AI technology, with a focus on areas such as machine learning, natural language processing, and computer vision. These research efforts have helped China to make significant strides in AI technology, with Chinese researchers publishing groundbreaking work in top AI conferences and journals.

Furthermore, China's investment in AI research and development has extended to the application of AI technology in various industries. Companies like Baidu, Alibaba, and Tencent have been at the forefront of developing AI-powered applications and services, ranging from autonomous vehicles and intelligent personal assistants to facial recognition technology and e-commerce recommendation systems. These companies have leveraged China's strong research capabilities and vast amounts of data to drive innovation and push the boundaries of AI technology.

Overall, China's investment in AI research and development has positioned the country as a global leader in artificial intelligence. With a strong focus on education, research, and application, China is well on its way to achieving its goal of becoming the world's dominant force in AI by 2030. By continuing to support and invest in AI technology, China is poised to shape the future of AI innovation and drive economic growth in the years to come.

AI Education and Talent Development

In order to achieve its goal of becoming the world leader in AI by 2030, China has recognized the importance of investing in AI education and talent development. The government has made significant investments in this area, focusing on improving educational programs, funding research initiatives, and promoting the development of AI applications. This strategic approach is aimed at cultivating a skilled workforce that can drive innovation and technological advancements in the field of artificial intelligence.

One key aspect of China's AI education strategy is the emphasis on integrating AI into the curriculum at all levels of education.

From primary schools to universities, students are being exposed to AI concepts and technologies to prepare them for the future workforce. In addition, the government has established specialized AI research institutes and centers of excellence to promote collaboration between academia, industry, and government in advancing AI research and development.

Companies like Baidu, Alibaba, and Tencent are leading the way in AI technology in China, driving innovation and pushing the boundaries of what is possible with artificial intelligence. These tech giants are actively involved in talent development initiatives, offering training programs, internships, and mentorship opportunities to nurture the next generation of AI experts. By partnering with academic institutions and research organizations, these companies are helping to bridge the gap between theory and practice in the field of AI.

In order to sustain its momentum in AI development, China is also focused on attracting top talent from around the world. The government has implemented policies to encourage skilled professionals to work in China, offering incentives such as research grants, funding for startups, and fast-track visa processing. This influx of international talent is helping to create a diverse and dynamic AI ecosystem in China, driving innovation and fostering collaboration on a global scale.

Overall, China's commitment to AI education and talent development is a key factor in its ambitious plan to become the world leader in artificial intelligence by 2030. By investing in educational programs, research initiatives, and talent recruitment efforts, China is laying the foundation for a sustainable and competitive AI industry that will drive economic growth and technological advancement in the years to come.

Chapter 3: Leading AI Companies in China

Baidu: Pioneer in AI Technology

Baidu, often referred to as the "Google of China," has been a pioneer in the field of artificial intelligence technology. Founded in 2000, Baidu has rapidly grown to become one of the leading tech companies in China, with a strong focus on AI research and development. The company has made significant investments in AI technology, positioning itself at the forefront of China's AI revolution.

One of the key areas where Baidu has excelled in AI technology is in natural language processing. The company's deep learning algorithms have enabled it to develop advanced speech recognition and language translation systems, which are widely used in its search engine and other products. Baidu's AI-powered virtual assistant, DuerOS, has also gained significant traction in the market, competing with global players like Amazon's Alexa and Apple's Siri.

In addition to its work in natural language processing, Baidu has also been a leader in computer vision technology. The company has developed cutting-edge image recognition algorithms, which are used in applications ranging from autonomous vehicles to facial recognition systems. Baidu's research in computer vision has helped to drive advancements in AI technology, making it a key player in China's AI ecosystem.

Furthermore, Baidu has been actively involved in the development of AI applications in healthcare, finance, and other industries. The company's AI-powered healthcare platform, Baidu Health, uses machine learning algorithms to provide personalized medical recommendations to users. In the finance sector, Baidu has developed AI systems for risk assessment and fraud detection, helping financial institutions to improve their decision-making processes.

Overall, Baidu's commitment to AI research and development has positioned it as a key player in China's AI revolution. As the country continues to invest heavily in AI technology, companies like Baidu will play a crucial role in driving innovation and shaping the future of the industry. With its expertise in natural language processing, computer vision, and AI applications, Baidu is well-positioned to lead China's charge towards becoming the world leader in AI by 2030.

Alibaba: Innovations in AI Applications

Alibaba, one of China's tech giants, has been at the forefront of innovation in artificial intelligence (AI) applications. With the Chinese government heavily investing in AI technology, companies like Alibaba have been able to push the boundaries of what is possible in the realm of AI. From improving online shopping experiences to revolutionizing supply chain management, Alibaba has been a key player in the advancement of AI technology in China.

One of the areas where Alibaba has made significant strides in AI applications is in the field of e-commerce. Through the use of AI algorithms, Alibaba has been able to personalize the shopping experience for its customers, recommend products based on their browsing history, and even predict future trends in consumer behavior. This has not only improved the overall shopping experience for consumers but has also increased sales for Alibaba's online platform.

In addition to e-commerce, Alibaba has also been utilizing AI technology in areas such as logistics and supply chain management. By implementing AI algorithms to optimize delivery routes, predict demand, and manage inventory, Alibaba has been able to streamline its operations and improve efficiency. This has led to cost savings for the company and faster delivery times for customers, further solidifying Alibaba's position as a leader in AI applications.

Furthermore, Alibaba has been investing heavily in research and development to further advance AI technology. Through partnerships with universities and research institutions, Alibaba has been able to stay at the cutting edge of AI innovation. This has allowed the company to develop new AI applications and solutions that have the potential to revolutionize various industries in China and beyond.

Overall, Alibaba's innovations in AI applications have not only propelled the company to the forefront of the tech industry in China but have also helped to drive the country's ambition to become the world leader in AI by 2030. With continued investments in research, development, and application of AI technology, Alibaba is poised to continue leading the way in AI innovation and shaping the future of technology in China and beyond.

Tencent: Advancements in AI Research

Tencent, one of China's leading technology companies, has been making significant advancements in AI research in recent years. With the Chinese government's strong investment in AI development, Tencent has been at the forefront of leveraging artificial intelligence to drive innovation and create new opportunities in various industries.

One of Tencent's key areas of focus in AI research is natural language processing. By developing advanced algorithms and models, Tencent has been able to improve the accuracy and efficiency of machine translation, speech recognition, and text analysis. This has enabled Tencent to enhance the user experience across its platforms and services, as well as to explore new applications of AI in communication and content creation.

In addition to natural language processing, Tencent has also been investing in computer vision technology. By training deep learning models on large datasets of images and videos, Tencent has been able to develop algorithms that can accurately identify and classify objects, scenes, and actions in visual data. This has enabled Tencent to enhance the capabilities of its products in areas such as image recognition, augmented reality, and autonomous driving.

Furthermore, Tencent has been actively collaborating with academic institutions and research organizations to advance AI research in China. By fostering partnerships with leading experts in the field, Tencent has been able to stay at the cutting edge of AI technology and contribute to the global AI research community. This collaborative approach has helped Tencent to attract top talent, explore new research directions, and accelerate the pace of AI innovation.

Overall, Tencent's advancements in AI research are a testament to China's ambition to become a world leader in artificial intelligence by 2030. By investing in education, research, and application, Tencent and other leading Chinese companies are driving the development of AI technology and shaping the future of industries worldwide. With Tencent's continued efforts in AI research, China is well-positioned to achieve its goal of leading the AI revolution in the coming decade.

Chapter 4: Challenges and Opportunities in China's AI Evolution

Ethical and Regulatory Issues in AI Development

Ethical and regulatory issues in AI development are crucial considerations for China as it strives to become the world leader in artificial intelligence by 2030. The Chinese government has made significant investments in AI, with a focus on education, research, and application. Companies like Baidu, Alibaba, and Tencent are leading the charge in AI technology development in China, but with this rapid advancement comes a host of ethical and regulatory challenges that must be addressed.

One of the key ethical issues in AI development is the potential for bias in algorithms. AI systems are only as good as the data they are trained on, and if that data is biased or flawed, it can lead to discriminatory outcomes. China must ensure that its AI systems are fair and unbiased, taking steps to address any inherent biases in the data and algorithms that power these systems.

Another ethical concern is the impact of AI on jobs and the workforce. As AI technology advances, there is a fear that automation will lead to widespread job loss and economic disruption. China must consider the social implications of AI development and work to mitigate any negative consequences for workers who may be displaced by automation.

On the regulatory front, China must establish clear guidelines and standards for the development and deployment of AI technology. This includes issues related to data privacy, cybersecurity, and intellectual property rights. China's regulatory framework must strike a balance between fostering innovation and protecting the rights and interests of individuals and businesses.

Overall, navigating the ethical and regulatory challenges of AI development will be critical for China as it seeks to achieve its goal of becoming the global leader in artificial intelligence by 2030. By addressing these issues head-on and implementing robust ethical and regulatory frameworks, China can ensure that its AI revolution is not only technologically advanced but also socially responsible and sustainable in the long run.

International Collaboration and Competition in AI

In the rapidly evolving field of artificial intelligence (AI), international collaboration and competition play a crucial role in shaping the future of the industry. As China continues on its path to becoming a global leader in AI by 2030, the country is actively engaging with other nations to exchange knowledge, resources, and expertise in this cutting-edge technology. This collaboration not only fosters innovation but also strengthens diplomatic ties between countries, paving the way for a more interconnected and technologically advanced world.

China's AI revolution has been fueled by heavy investments from the government, with a particular focus on education, research, and application. The country's top tech companies, such as Baidu, Alibaba, and Tencent, have emerged as key players in the AI landscape, driving innovation and pushing the boundaries of what is possible with this transformative technology. These companies are not only competing with each other but also collaborating on various projects to accelerate the development of AI technologies and applications.

One of the key drivers of China's AI ambition is the government's strategic plan to leverage AI as a tool for economic growth and national development. By investing in research and development, talent acquisition, and infrastructure, China aims to build a thriving AI ecosystem that will drive innovation, create new industries, and enhance the country's global competitiveness. This forward-thinking approach has positioned China as a frontrunner in the race to 2030, with ambitious goals to lead the world in AI research, development, and deployment.

As China's AI sector continues to expand and mature, the country is increasingly looking to international partners to collaborate on joint research projects, share best practices, and explore new business opportunities. By fostering relationships with leading AI companies and research institutions around the world, China is able to tap into a global network of expertise and talent, driving innovation and accelerating the pace of technological advancement. This spirit of collaboration not only benefits China's AI industry but also contributes to the broader goal of building a more inclusive and interconnected global AI community.

In conclusion, international collaboration and competition are essential components of China's AI revolution, driving innovation, fostering partnerships, and advancing the country's ambitious goals for AI leadership by 2030. By engaging with global partners, sharing knowledge and resources, and working together to push the boundaries of AI technology, China is positioning itself as a key player in the future of artificial intelligence. As the race to 2030 heats up, China's commitment to collaboration and competition will be instrumental in shaping the future of AI and driving continued progress in this dynamic and rapidly evolving field.

Potential Impact of China's AI Dominance on Global Economy

China's rapid advancement in artificial intelligence (AI) technology has the potential to have a significant impact on the global economy. As the Chinese government continues to heavily invest in AI, focusing on education, research, and application, companies like Baidu, Alibaba, and Tencent are at the forefront of AI technology in China. This dominance in AI has the potential to reshape the global economic landscape by 2030.

One potential impact of China's AI dominance on the global economy is the increased productivity and efficiency in various industries. With the integration of AI technology in sectors such as manufacturing, healthcare, and finance, Chinese companies are able to streamline processes, reduce costs, and improve overall performance. This increased efficiency could lead to greater competitiveness on a global scale, potentially disrupting traditional industries and creating new opportunities for growth.

Furthermore, China's AI dominance could also lead to the development of new business models and industries. As Chinese companies continue to innovate and push the boundaries of AI technology, they may create entirely new markets and products that have the potential to revolutionize the global economy. This could lead to new job opportunities, increased investment, and overall economic growth both in China and around the world.

Another potential impact of China's AI dominance on the global economy is the shift in geopolitical power dynamics. As China solidifies its position as a leader in AI technology, it may have greater influence on international policies, trade agreements, and global standards. This could potentially reshape the balance of power between countries and impact how global economies interact with each other in the future.

Overall, the potential impact of China's AI dominance on the global economy is vast and far-reaching. As China continues to invest in AI and push the boundaries of technological innovation, the world may see significant changes in how industries operate, how businesses compete, and how countries interact with each other on a global scale. It is crucial for stakeholders to closely monitor China's AI revolution and its implications on the global economy to stay ahead of the curve in this rapidly evolving landscape.

Chapter 5: Future Outlook for China's AI Industry

Predictions for China's Position in AI by 2030

In the race to become a global leader in artificial intelligence (AI) by 2030, China has positioned itself as a formidable contender. The Chinese government has made significant investments in AI, with a focus on education, research, and application. This strategic approach has allowed China to rapidly advance in the field of AI, with companies like Baidu, Alibaba, and Tencent leading the charge in developing cutting-edge technology.

By 2030, it is predicted that China will have solidified its position as a dominant force in AI on the world stage. The government's continued support for AI research and development, coupled with the innovative initiatives of leading tech companies, will propel China to the forefront of AI technology. This will not only benefit China's economy but also have far-reaching implications for industries around the globe.

One key factor driving China's AI revolution is the country's vast pool of data. With a population of over 1.4 billion people and a rapidly growing digital economy, China has access to massive amounts of data that can be used to train AI algorithms. This data advantage gives China a competitive edge in developing AI applications across a wide range of industries, from healthcare and finance to transportation and manufacturing.

In addition to data, China's focus on AI education and talent development will also play a crucial role in shaping the country's position in AI by 2030. The government has implemented initiatives to nurture a new generation of AI experts, while leading tech companies are investing in AI research centers and collaborations with top universities. This emphasis on talent development will ensure that China has the skilled workforce necessary to drive innovation and maintain its competitive edge in AI technology.

Overall, the outlook for China's position in AI by 2030 is bright. With strong government support, a thriving tech industry, and a wealth of data at its disposal, China is poised to lead the way in AI innovation in the coming years. As the country continues to invest in AI research and talent development, we can expect to see China solidify its role as a global leader in artificial intelligence by 2030.

Potential Implications of China's AI Revolution on Society

China's AI revolution has the potential to have far-reaching implications on society, both within China and globally. As the Chinese government continues to invest heavily in AI research and development, the country is poised to become a world leader in artificial intelligence by the year 2030. This ambitious goal has led to a rapid growth in AI technology, with companies like Baidu, Alibaba, and Tencent leading the charge in innovation and application.

One potential implication of China's AI revolution on society is the impact on the job market. With the rise of automation and AI technology, many traditional jobs may be at risk of being replaced by machines. This could lead to widespread unemployment and a shift in the workforce towards more specialized, AI-related roles. However, it also presents opportunities for new industries and job creation in the AI sector.

Another potential implication of China's AI revolution is the impact on privacy and data security. As AI technology becomes more advanced, the collection and analysis of personal data will become more prevalent. This raises concerns about how this data will be used and protected, as well as the potential for privacy breaches and data theft. It will be important for the Chinese government and companies to develop robust regulations and security measures to address these concerns.

Furthermore, the widespread adoption of AI technology in China could have significant implications for healthcare, transportation, and other industries. AI has the potential to revolutionize healthcare by improving diagnosis and treatment outcomes, as well as making healthcare more accessible and affordable. In transportation, AI technology can lead to more efficient and safer systems, with the potential for self-driving cars and smart transportation networks.

Overall, the implications of China's AI revolution on society are vast and complex. While there are potential risks and challenges to navigate, there are also immense opportunities for innovation, growth, and progress. As China continues on its path to becoming a global leader in AI by 2030, it will be essential for the government, companies, and society as a whole to work together to ensure that the benefits of AI technology are realized while mitigating any potential negative impacts.

Recommendations for Businesses and Governments in Response to China's AI Ambition

As China continues its rapid advancements in artificial intelligence (AI) technology, businesses and governments around the world must take note of the implications and challenges that come with China's AI ambition. In order to effectively compete and collaborate with Chinese companies and researchers, it is crucial for businesses and governments to make strategic decisions and investments in AI technology.

First and foremost, businesses must prioritize investment in AI research and development in order to stay competitive in the global market. Companies like Baidu, Alibaba, and Tencent have already established themselves as leaders in AI technology in China, and companies in other countries must follow suit in order to keep up with the rapidly evolving landscape of AI innovation. By investing in AI research and development, businesses can stay ahead of the curve and continue to push the boundaries of what is possible with AI technology.

Governments also play a crucial role in responding to China's AI ambition. In order to foster innovation and growth in the AI sector, governments must invest in education and training programs to develop a skilled workforce that is capable of working with AI technology. By supporting AI education initiatives and providing resources for AI research, governments can help to create a robust ecosystem for AI innovation that will benefit both businesses and society as a whole.

Additionally, governments must also prioritize data privacy and security in response to China's AI ambition. With the increasing use of AI technology in various sectors, it is crucial for governments to establish clear regulations and guidelines for the ethical use of AI and the protection of sensitive data. By implementing strong data privacy laws and regulations, governments can ensure that AI technology is used responsibly and ethically, while also protecting the rights and privacy of individuals.

Overall, the rise of China's AI ambition presents both opportunities and challenges for businesses and governments around the world. By making strategic investments in AI research and development, prioritizing education and training programs, and establishing strong data privacy regulations, businesses and governments can effectively respond to China's AI ambition and position themselves for success in the global AI market.

Chapter 6: Conclusion

Key Takeaways from China's AI Revolution

China's AI revolution is well underway, with the government making significant investments in education, research, and application of artificial intelligence. The goal is to become the world leader in AI by 2030, and the country is well on its way to achieving that goal. Companies like Baidu, Alibaba, and

Tencent are leading the charge in developing cutting-edge AI technology that is revolutionizing industries across the board.

One key takeaway from China's AI revolution is the government's heavy investment in education. China has recognized the importance of developing a skilled workforce that is well-versed in AI technology. The government has implemented programs to train students in AI-related fields, ensuring that the country has the talent it needs to drive innovation in the industry.

Another key takeaway is the focus on research and development. China has established numerous research institutes and centers dedicated to advancing AI technology. These institutions are conducting groundbreaking research that is pushing the boundaries of what is possible with artificial intelligence. This commitment to R&D is a key factor in China's rapid advancement in the field.

One of the most notable aspects of China's AI revolution is the application of AI technology across various industries. Companies like Baidu, Alibaba, and Tencent are leading the way in implementing AI solutions in sectors such as healthcare, finance, and transportation. These companies are leveraging AI to improve efficiency, increase productivity, and drive innovation in their respective industries.

Overall, China's AI revolution is a testament to the country's commitment to becoming a global leader in artificial intelligence. With heavy investments in education, research, and application, China is well-positioned to achieve its goal of dominating the AI market by 2030. The advancements being made by companies like Baidu, Alibaba, and Tencent are paving the way for a future where AI technology plays a crucial role in shaping the world economy.

Final Thoughts on the Road to 2030

As we come to the end of our exploration into China's AI Revolution and the Road to 2030, it is clear that the country is well on its way to becoming a global leader in artificial intelligence. The Chinese government has made significant investments in AI, with a strong focus on education, research, and application. This has laid a solid foundation for the rapid development and adoption of AI technologies in various sectors.

Companies like Baidu, Alibaba, and Tencent are leading the charge in AI innovation in China. Their cutting-edge technologies and strategic partnerships are pushing the boundaries of what is possible in the field of artificial intelligence. Through their collaboration with government agencies, research institutions, and other industry players, these companies are driving the advancement of AI in China at an unprecedented pace.

As we look ahead to 2030, it is clear that China's AI ambition is not just a lofty goal but a strategic imperative. The country's leadership in AI technology will have far-reaching implications for its economy, society, and global influence. By harnessing the power of artificial intelligence, China aims to enhance its competitiveness, drive innovation, and improve the quality of life for its citizens.

It is important for stakeholders, both within and outside of China, to closely monitor the country's progress in AI development. Understanding China's AI strategy and the key players driving this revolution will be crucial for anyone looking to stay ahead in the rapidly evolving field of artificial intelligence.

In conclusion, China's AI Revolution is a testament to the country's unwavering commitment to innovation and technological advancement. By leveraging its resources, talent, and strategic partnerships, China is well-positioned to become the world leader in AI by 2030. The road ahead may be challenging, but with the right vision and determination, China is poised to shape the future of artificial intelligence for years to come.